7 LOVE KEYS TO A SUCCESSFUL MARRIAGE

Principles for a Lasting Relationship

by
SHAWN & CALEEN HOWARD

7 Love Keys To A Successful Marriage
Principles for a Lasting Relationship
by Shawn & Caleen Howard

Printed in the United States of America.

ISBN 9781498438568

Scripture quotations taken from the English Standard Version (ESV). Copyright © 2001 by Crossway, a publishing ministry of Good News Publishers. Used by permission. All rights reserved.

www.xulonpress.com

Table of Contents

Dedication

We would like to dedicate this book to our children: Malachi, Caleb, and Jordynn-Renee. You are truly God's gift to us and our prayer is the legacy of love we are building through our marriage and within our family will live on through each of you for generations to come. We love you from the bottom of our hearts and we know each of you will be a great blessing to the world.

We would also like to dedicate this book to the "Couples Group of 1999" *(Glen & Nordia, Shaun & Tanya, Garfield & Michelle, Gillian & Roland "Boz", Gerry & Deon)* who took the plunge along with us and also tied their knots in 1999 to embark on this great journey called marriage.

Without your love and support in the early stages, who knows where we would have ended up. Also to Nadine & Kirk and Dion & Natasha who tapped in as great friends throughout the journey. Our prayer is that you all experience life-long success in your marriages as well.

Acknowledgments

To our parents Andre & Annette Howard and James & Brenda (dec.) Clarke: we thank you for the example of your marriages that have helped shape our relationship in a manner that reflects honor, love, and respect.

To our siblings: Dexter, Amy, Nicole, Kevin, Chantel, and all of our extended family for being great supporters of our marriage, children, and all of our endeavors.

To Grace (our official "matchmaker"), Gillian, Marva, Andrew, and all of the friends who have supported us over the years.

To our church family: Life Changers Church, and all of the couples that we have had the honor of counseling, marrying, and mentoring: We love and appreciate you all!

Foreword

ishop Shawn and Rev. Caleen Howard have had so many successful stories through their years together in ministry and marriage. They have been called of God to help shape and disciple lives, not only in Toronto, Canada, but the world. This book is the debut outside of their parish... So, get ready to have your marriage inspired.

I have read the manuscript and found it easy to read. It is with great joy in my heart that I write this foreword for a young couple that I admire and have watched growing into becoming a model couple and leader in today's culture.

As you continue to read this book you will know why they have become a model couple. Just to get your thoughts going, they will share 7 LOVE KEYS TO A SUCCESSFUL MARRIAGE which are Principles for a Lasting Relationship however, there are two things they never mentioned as secrets which indeed are. They started their married journey truly committed to God and the institution of marriage and they partnered with a couples support group called, "Couples Group of 1999".

Today, as a result of what they have learnt on their marital journey, the Spirit of the Lord has prompted them to share it with you. They could have said no to the Holy Spirit, but they knew that it would cost them more to disobey than to obey.

They do not approach this writing as experts, but as "another beggar helping another beggar along their marital journey."

In this book you will learn or be reminded about 7 love keys. If you will apply them, they will strengthen your relationship and bring you closer together as a couple. These are 7 practical truths that no marriage can survive without. If you would study these 7 keys, Friendship, Communication, Teamwork, Intimacy, Commitment, Forgiveness and Spiritual Unity and keep them in your mind and practice them daily in your marriage, I can assure you your marriage journey will become more fun traveling.

In my opinion, one of the greatest and most important part of the book is the chapter dealing with Spiritual Unity. In there they have outlined another secret that connects all the seven keys. It is prayer. If you are weak in any of the first 6, let me encourage you to practice the prayer therapy. Prayer will help you fulfill the other six keys.

The 7 Love Keys to A Successful Marriage is a must read for you...And read together to get the best results.

Dr. Daniel J. Vassell, Author

"The Love Factor" & "Living the Blessed-Filled Life Now"

Letter

*D*ear Reader,.

Congratulations on beginning the journey of discovering *7 Love Keys to a Successful Marriage*!

This book is an instructional guide intended for couples to enjoy together. We encourage you to approach this book in the following ways:

- Read each chapter together
- Read the **Reference Scriptures**
- Answer the **Reflection Questions** at the end of each chapter
- Spend time sharing answers and reflection points with your spouse

- Pray together before moving on to the next chapter.

Your marriage is an important relationship; and every investment made to strengthen the bond between you and your spouse will yield wonderful returns.

Enjoy the Journey!

Shawn & Caleen Howard

Introduction/Preface

W hen you think of the word "marriage", what are the thoughts that come to mind? Some see marriage as a contract, while others see marriage as a big wedding day, and still others see marriage as an expression of love. Whatever your thoughts or ideas are about marriage, it is ultimately a type of relationship that is considered valuable and held in high regard. Relationships develop over a period of time through dedication, faithfulness, trust, confidence, and love, ultimately becoming beautiful masterpieces built with the ingredients of personalities, character, and experiences through the choice we have to pursue what we feel happening inside of us. The truth is, relationships grow and mature into friendships, partnerships, companionships, and even a marriage. Marriage is a binding commitment between a man and a woman intended by God for the mutual joy, help, and comfort given to one another in prosperity and adversity. The beautiful thing about marriage is it is a mélange/mixture of different types of relationships all joined together in a vessel made for transport. Think of marriage as a ship as you embark on a journey, a pilgrimage, a voyage, or an excursion taking you and your spouse from one point to another that leads to a destination traveled in time with goals and decisions made through love and unity. Marriage is special. With commitment and dedication, it has the potential to become a lasting legacy of love that will be an example for many generations to follow.

What is love? How do you define love? Our understanding of love is based on two main components: examples and experience. Most people define love based on what they have seen as examples of love and what they have experienced as expressions of love. You may have an image of love or an ideal marriage you think is perfect, or your views of marriage may be formed through movies or television shows that have given you a concept based on someone else's vision of the "love interests" in the production. Or perhaps you have admired and formed definitions of the perfect relationship based on observing other couples appearing to have elements in their marriage that you long for—"Did you see how they looked at each other?" "I love the way he treats her" "She really supports her man" "Wow, those two have a great relationship." Most people want to be loved and experience joy, happiness, and contentment along with adding meaning to their lives with positive feelings and desires. Regardless of how many different concepts of love you may admire or aspire toward, the greatest experience of love for *you* will be how *your* marriage is built and nurtured through the experiences you have on the ship with your spouse.

Now before you set sail, every ship needs a captain—a navigator who knows the course and is confident of the direction to take and the turns to make in the journey of life. Who better to have as the captain of the ship than the ultimate Creator Himself? Through spiritual guidance and direction, couples will learn how to approach their relationship with a clearer understanding of love along this journey called marriage. Paul wrote to the Corinthian church in 1 Corinthians 13:4-8 (ESV):

> Love is patient and kind; love does not envy or boast; it is not arrogant or rude. It does not insist on its own way; it is not irritable or resentful; it does not rejoice at wrongdoing, but rejoices with the truth. Love bears all things, believes all things, hopes all things, endures all things. Love never ends.

It is the love between you and your spouse that will help you to overcome every obstacle, challenge, and experience you face on this journey.

As you read this book, you may not have set sail as yet, or you may have just left the dock, or perhaps you have been on the sea traveling for quite some time. No matter where you are in your marriage, we have written this book to share *Seven Love Keys to a Successful Marriage.*

These seven keys emerge from four of the relational ancient Greek expressions of love: *Philos, eros, pragma, and agapeo or agape.* The other relational expression of love, storge or *storgē* is a natural familiar/family love expressed from a parent to a child. C.S. Lewis in *"The Four Loves"* explores the nature of love from a Christian and philosophical perspective through thought experiments, and distinguishes between "need/gift love" and "pleasure" from the Greek definitions.

Philos *(philia)* – Is a brotherly/friendship love, fondness, or bond between two people who share common values, interests, activities, and experiences. *Philos* steadily grows out of companionship like a building being constructed stone by stone as it develops a deep sense of appreciation for the other person. For this reason, when close friends are separated for a while and reunited, they will often say, "it is like we picked up exactly where we left off." *Philos* is half about circumstances, and half about the commitment of two people to one another; it says, "I love who we are together." According to Lewis this friendship love is "the least biological, organic, instinctive, gregarious and necessary...the least natural of loves." Philos love generally grows over time except in the case of some kind of betrayal.

Eros (erōs)- is obviously the root word for "erotic", but it does not describe sexual love only; it actually describes all emotional love and the feeling of love. *Eros* love is the insatiable sexual desire and passion to be near the target of this love. The exciting, passionate, butterflies, and nervous feelings that sweeps over people in the appropriate circumstances. This is the love that says, "I love how you make me feel." As an emotion, *eros* changes, sometimes suddenly. Remember that it is entirely based on circumstances and on the target of its emotion.

Pragma – is a mature love often seen between couples who have been married for a long time. The practicality and realism of this pragmatic love often aides the longevity of a relationship. This type of love carries the notion of one person being of service or usefulness to the other, and also translates to having expectations in a partner and of the relationship. Individuals expressing this love tend to select and reject partners based on what they perceive desirable, compatible traits. Pragmatic lovers want to find value in their partners, and ultimately want to work with their partner to reach a common goal.

Agapeo (Agápē) – is a self-sacrificing, magnanimous, altruistic love which entirely describes the lover, and has nothing whatsoever to do with the one loved. Agape love, in its purest form, requires no payment or favor in response because it produces more pleasure from giving rather than receiving. This lack of input from the recipient makes it possible for us to love unconditionally even though we may not like them, some of their habits, or the situation they have put us in. The most common word for God's love for us is agape, and the love we are instructed to have for one another. *Agape* love is not in any way dependent on circumstances; it says, "I love you because I choose/commit to." Although many people marry out of *eros* love alone, they make vows that speak of commitment despite any circumstance "richer/ poorer, better/worse, sickness/health." This kind of love is about a commitment to the best for another, no matter what emotions or feelings exist. It is a love freely given, and freely committed.

Through countless hours and many years providing relationship and marriage counseling and advice, we have discovered many people seek foundational principles and examples of how to make their marriage last. Society has celebrated divorce and has offered many damaging outlets for relationship dysfunction and failures; but we believe that marriage is still the number one foundation for the family, community, and the betterment of the world. After twenty years of relationship and sixteen years of marriage, we have grown and faced some challenges that could have taken us out—literally meaning the end of our marriage—but the love we share for one another will always have the best of us, not by luck or chance, but by choice. The journey isn't easy and we are still learning new things about our relationship on a daily, weekly, monthly, and yearly basis, but we choose to seek and find ways to love each other more. Along this journey we have discovered principles that will educate, enlighten, and empower your marriage to last a lifetime; our prayer is you will use these keys to unlock and activate the hidden treasures that lie within your own marriage. "Till death do us part" is not a life sentence, but a beautiful love story. It's time to start loving!

"Till death do us part" is not a life
sentence, but a beautiful love story.
It's time to start loving!

Key #1:

Friendship ("Ride or Die")

Philia Love

Friendship is a relationship of mutual affection between two or more people. It is a stronger form of an interpersonal bond than an association that connects people through a commitment to loving and respecting each other despite the challenges you may face.

*F*riendship is one of the most important keys to maintaining a successful marriage. Most people have journeyed through life establishing many different friendships along the way. Some have maintained close relationships with people they've known since childhood, while others establish close friends through special interest groups, clubs, schools, workplaces, or even neighborhoods. No matter how the relationship began, true friendships stand the test of time and are more precious than valuable items we could ever acquire. As the old saying goes, "True friends are hard to find", but when you do find one, they should be loved and cherished. A true friend is someone with whom you share common interests, experiences, and goals; someone with whom you feel completely comfortable; a person with whom you are honest and transparent; someone with whom you can laugh and cry. A person who can tell you the truth even when it hurts because you know they have your best interest at heart. When you speak to this person, you lose track of time because the conversation is a natural dialogue of shared interests, understanding, and respect for each other's thoughts and views.

A true friend has your back in the good and bad times ("ride or die"); someone you can depend on and with whom you can be yourself. When people are more connected to you for what they can receive, a true friend cares about what they can contribute to the relationship. So how does friendship tie into the marriage relationship? Many couples fail to realize while you may have friends outside of a marriage, the friendship within the marriage is one of the keys to true companionship. Being a friend to your spouse means you look out for their interests-you support your spouse-you cheer them on when they are achieving their goals; you weep with them when they are going through rough times, and rejoice at their victories all while enjoying each other's company, and the ability to be oneself, and make mistakes without fear of judgment from each other. A heart of true friendship would never intentionally cause pain or hurt that will betray or disrespect a relationship so honorable; and being a friend to each other is a natural commitment to the long-lasting development and continuation of the relationship.

Our relationship began at eighteen years old when a mutual friend first introduced us to each other. It felt easier to build friendships back then because of the natural flow of social development and interaction at that time. Teens naturally built and maintained friendships based on common interests and positive networks. High school was a great starting point for us to build a real friendship that has grown and continues to grow through our entire relationship. While our personalities and interests differ in some ways, we realize in many ways we are similar and share so many common goals and dreams, which has deepened our bond and acceptance of each other.

The friendship we've built has helped us to work through our differences and has been a foundation that guides us through times of disagreements and difficult challenges. We have found that it is easier to forgive and move on passed offences because of how deeply rooted the friendship aspect of our relationship has been. Being a friend to your spouse means out of everyone in the world, you will be there till the end. The old sitcom "Golden Girls" had a jingle for the opening of the show:

"Thank you for being a friend, traveled down the road and back again, your heart is true, you're a pal and a confident, and if you threw a party and invited everyone you knew, you would see the greatest gift would be from me, and the card attached would say, "Thank you for being a friend."

Although the sentiments of this song prove true to different types of friendships one may have, being able to have a close relationship like this with your spouse will truly increase your bond.

While being attracted to someone may draw you into the relationship, the friendship that is developed over time will be a significant key that will keep the relationship healthy. Begin to see your spouse as your friend—a person who you can laugh, cry, talk, vent, and share every moment of your life.

People have asked the question, "Why would I want to marry my friend?" because they wonder if marrying a friend is a good idea for fear of complicating a friendship or becoming romantically involved with someone with whom they've built a trusting, genuine relationship with no strings attached, but the truth is building a friendship before and during marriage becomes a wonderful foundation for the deeper relationship developed along the journey. The real question is: why become romantically involved with someone with whom you have not developed a trusting and genuine friendship? Couples who neglect the friendship aspect of the relationship will face the challenges that come from the lack of trust and the genuine openness needed for positive relationship building. Building friendship within your marriage is a *key* that will unlock trust, affection, sympathy, understanding, and compassion. Start investing into the friendship element of your marriage and you will begin to see the relationship blossom.

Building friendship within your marriage is a key that will unlock trust, affection, sympathy, understanding, and compassion.

Reflection Scriptures:

Ephesians 4:2-3 (ESV):

"Be completely humble and gentle; be patient, bearing with one another in love. Make every effort to keep the unity of the Spirit through the bond of peace."

John 15:13 (ESV):

"Greater love has no one than this, that he lay down his life for his friends."

Reflection Questions:

1. **Do you view your spouse as a friend? If not, why? If Yes, describe three ways in which they are a friend.**

_____

_____

_____

_____

_____

_____

_____

_____

2. In what ways have you been a friend to your spouse?

_____

_____

_____

_____

_____

3. List three ways you can develop a healthier friendship with your spouse.

_____

_____

_____

_____

_____

Prayer: Father, thank you for the key of friendship and for helping us to understand its importance within our relationship. Help us to better nourish, treasure, and develop our friendship so that we can experience true companionship in Jesus' name. Amen.

Key #2:

Communication (Talk About It)

Philia Love

ommunication is the act or process of using words, sounds, signs, or behaviors to express or exchange information or to express your ideas, thoughts, feelings, etc., to someone else.

Have you ever heard the saying, "absence makes the heart grow fonder"? This particular saying is a quote stating the length of time separated from the person you love creates a deeper sense of love and appreciation for them. This statement means a lot to a couple in love where great communication skills are used. This statement can mean something completely different for another couple that struggles with communicating with their spouse. An absence from their spouse is like an emotional, physical, and mental break! We're sure there is someone reading this right now that will agree with this statement. It is like you couldn't wait to get away from the person, because when you are with them the poor (or lack of) communication you experience literally drives you crazy. A comedian once said, *"Before marriage, a man will lie awake all night thinking about something you said: after marriage, he'll fall asleep before you finish saying it."* Couples that communicate well with each other seem to be much happier in their relationships; while couples who lack effective communication struggle in their relationship privately and publicly. Whatever the struggle is in the relationship, if not looked after, will publicly manifest. It's only a matter of time.

We've all heard the saying, "communication is the key to a successful relationship", and while many agree with this statement, it must be noted, "effective communication is the key to a successful relationship." Have you ever tried to explain your thoughts to your spouse and they didn't understand you? The feeling of being misunderstood combined with the response from your spouse can be totally frustrating and exhausting. This type of frustration has caused many couples to cease communicating altogether or to even walk away from their marriages. A relationship will blossom like a flower when it is watered with positive communication; and this can be best achieved when both individuals take the time to listen and understand each other.

Marriage can be like ESL (English as a Second Language), but like any student studying a new language; it will take time, patience, and a commitment to learning.

While everyone communicates differently, it is the approach to listening and understanding that brings harmony to the communication flow. Communicating can be difficult, especially when you're speaking two different languages. Marriage can be like ESL (English as a Second Language), but like any student studying a new language; it will take time, patience, and a commitment to learning. Many of the challenges couples face occur because husband and wife are speaking two different languages and communicate with two different concepts of speaking, listening, and comprehension. Oftentimes the intentions and true meaning of what either person is trying to communicate gets lost in the midst of frustration, stress, and confusion, which escalates into endless quarrels, fights, and misunderstandings.

Negative communication can bring out the worst in a person. Communication that is driven by negative emotions or reactions become toxic because it focuses more on negative feelings rather than facts. When couples focus on proving, "who's right" from "who's wrong", or take a combative approach to every circumstance, it makes interacting with your spouse undesirable.

Those who bottle up their feelings exercise non-verbal communication, which can also have a negative impact on the relationship. Spouses who keep silent and refrain from expressing or sharing how they feel or expressing how their spouse may have hurt them will generate a build-up of unexpressed anger and resentment. Many couples disagree or argue about past experiences and tend to rehash issues and circumstances in order to build fighting ammo for their defense; but taking this approach to communicating only indicates the past issues were never discussed in a way that brought the necessary closure to the situation and drives you further and further apart. Bringing closure through sharing with each other will be positive steps toward healthy interactions with your spouse. Dr. Adrian Rogers, former pastor and evangelistic leader of Love Worth Finding Ministries wrote, "Marriage Counselors agree: Most, if not all, marriage problems are rooted in poor communication. We often act in our marriages as though we are soloists, singing alone and beholden to nobody. But marriage is a duet, not a solo. And the Song of Solomon shows us a real life marriage filled with the music of intimate, personal, and open communication."

Couples who learn to embrace the communication key within their marriage make a commitment to learning how the other person expresses, processes, and receives information; and each person approaches discussions with those traits in mind. Effective communication adds to the intimacy in a relationship; knowing the other person "gets you" strengthens the bond the both of you share, and creates a sense of mutual respect and positive energy. Strive to strengthen the communication skills with your spouse by speaking and listening in a way that creates a healthy exchange of information. This is the way to truly bring out the best in the relationship and each other. Words of affirmation, compliments, words of support, paying attention, and contributing to discussions will not only let your spouse know you are interested in what they have to say, but will open the door for them to speak and listen to you as well.

In Dr. Gary Chapman's book The Five Love Languages, he writes about the importance of expressing love in a way your spouse can understand. He explains that each person has a specific love language and communication with your spouse becomes more effective when it is approached from his/her love language. Chapman's five emotional love languages are: Words of Affirmation, Quality Time, Gifts, Acts of Service, and Personal Touch.

Through different channels of communication couples will begin to feel free to open up and share everything. Open the door to your spouse for a mutual expression of your deepest thoughts, emotions, and concerns, because a closed door to your spouse emotionally will eventually lead to a shutting away of physical connection as well. If you continue to learn and embrace each other's language, communication will become easier and will develop into enjoyable exchanges ultimately building anticipation for every opportunity to spend time sharing with your spouse. Challenge each other to deepen the lines of communication within your marriage, and create a safe place for open and honest conversations to take place. Couples can begin to strengthen their communication by using the following steps:

1. Speak openly and honestly with respect for each other's thoughts and feelings.
2. Listen and pay attention.
3. Repeat what you heard or how you interpreted what was said.
4. Seek for clarification.
5. Respond by sharing your thoughts or answering the questions.
6. Approach interaction with a positive attitude.

Take consideration in applying these steps, and you will begin to see the communication aspect of your relationship improve. *"Ultimately the bond of all companionship, whether in marriage or in friendship, is conversation."*
- **Oscar Wilde**

Reflection Scriptures:

Colossians 4:6 (ESV):
"Let your speech always be gracious, seasoned with salt, so that you may know how you ought to answer each person."

Proverbs 15:1 (ESV):
"A soft answer turns away wrath, but a harsh word stirs up anger."

Reflection Questions:

1. **Do you communicate effectively with your spouse? If not, why?**

_____

_____

_____

_____

_____

_____

_____

2. **How well does your spouse communicate to you? Discuss the difference between effective vs. non-effective communication.**

_____

_____

_____

_____

_____

3. List three ways that you can build a more effective communication style with each other.

_____

_____

_____

_____

_____

_____

_____

Prayer: Father, thank you for the key of communication. Just as you take the time to communicate to your children by speaking through your word and listening to our prayers; teach us how to communicate with each other in a manner that strengthens our bond in Jesus' Name. Amen.

Key #3:

Teamwork (We're on the Same Team)
Philia Love

*M*arriage is a partnership requiring team-work. From planning a wedding, to paying bills, cleaning a house, to managing children, when you get married you enlist to be part of a team. Any good coach knows in order to develop a successful team, you have to first discover each player's strengths, weak-nesses, background, and past experiences; such is the same with marriage.

In order to win at the game of marriage, the players involved must develop respect, love, and appreciation for their teammate. Your spouse is your teammate; he/she is not your enemy. The enemy of the team is anything you allow to come to divide the marriage or separate you as a couple. Zig Ziglar, an American author and motivational speaker said, *"Many marriages would be better if the hus-band and the wife clearly understood that they are on the same side."* Among the many reasons for separation or divorce, the most common causes are: infidelity, communication breakdown, physical/psychological/emotional abuse, financial issues, and sexual incompatibility.

From our experience counseling and helping couples, we have found while many couples deal with a few of the obstacles mentioned, the the most common challenge couples face in the area of teamwork is finances. Financial issues are among the top reasons for conflict and divorce in a marriage.

While the financial dynamic varies from one couple to the next, joining together in marriage means two lives come together to form one life, which includes combining and managing the resources. Some couples have issues with comparing salaries, while other couples deal with an unemployed spouse or simply different ways of managing and spending money. If not resolved, or a management strategy also addressing the other areas of risk, these potential issues can cause a lot of strain on a marriage and will require early intervention and planning to avoid breakup. Dr. Phil McGraw in his article Financial and Marital Harmony wrote, *"It's this simple: Money can ruin your marriage. In fact, it's the number one problem in marriages and the number one cause of divorce. People often underestimate the commitment in merging two lives together. The reason we fight most about money is because it's the most measurable. Sure, compromises also need to be made when it comes to issues of time, space and affection, but with money, the give and take is quantifiable."* To begin working as a team, take the time to discuss each other's strengths and weaknesses and develop strategies to face any of the challenges that may cause breakup. Acknowledge the issues that exist and then address them with support, where needed. One person's strength might be financial management, while the other person's strength might be organizing; one person might have a lot of patience, and the other person might be fun and spontaneous. All of the differences combined will make for a well-balanced team. When you begin to see your spouse as your "life's partner" and your "teammate for life", you can learn to appreciate them for who they are and the role they play in your relationship.

*When you begin to see your spouse as your
"life's partner" and your "teammate for life", you can
learn to appreciate them for who they are and
the role they play in your relationship.*

Behind every great team you will find a group of devoted fans. Some couples feel they can live independently without others, but having great networks of support for your marriage and your family is essential. Family members or friends who care about you and your spouse and care about the success of your relationship can serve as great support systems for your marriage. Having friends who won't only agree with you because of the relationship, but will tell you when you are wrong for the benefit of overcoming obstacles within your marriage are valuable people to have in your corner. While the relationship is built between the two individuals within the marriage, having the external support of family and friends can create walls of support around your marriage that will help to block out negative influences. Fawn Weaver, author of *The Happy Wives Club*

said, *"Surrounding yourself with others who build up your marriage rather than attempt to tear it down was a must."*

Couples who can build a network with other couples will often find new friends who add strength and great support to the relationship. Although every couple faces different challenges, many commonalities can be found amongst other couples who have either walked the same path before or who are experiencing similar challenges within their marriage. Positive associations will strengthen your relationship as you receive encouragement and motivation; you will, in turn, encourage and motivate others.

In the early stages of our marriage, seven couples that were newlyweds along with us (class of '99) developed a network to build avenues for social connections, marital support, and growth. The group served as a great help for us through the first few years of our marriage because we realized some of the growing pains we were experiencing in our marriage were similar to what other couples were experiencing. Through that outlet of sharing and connecting with other couples, we learned positive coping skills for many of the disagreements and challenges we faced along the journey. Having this community of friends became such a blessing to our lives so much, and we are still friends with many of those couples to this day as we have grown and experienced life together. A few of these couples have even become Godparents to our children and we are so grateful to have made these life-long friendships.

Couples who work as a team and understand their roles within their marriage live in a greater level of harmony. Through the following scripture, the Bible highlights the foundational roles for husbands and wives as a basis for the love and respect we should have for each other as a team:

Ephesians 5:22-33 (ESV):

> *"Wives, submit to your own husbands, as to the Lord. For the husband is the head of the wife even as Christ is the head of the church, his body, and is himself its Savior. Now as the church submits to Christ, so also wives should submit in everything to*

their husbands. Husbands, love your wives, as Christ loved the church and gave himself up for her, that he might sanctify her, having cleansed her by the washing of water with the word, so that he might present the church to himself in splendour, without spot or wrinkle or any such thing, that she might be holy and without blemish. In the same way husbands should love their wives as their own bodies. He who loves his wife loves himself. For no one ever hated his own flesh, but nourishes and cherishes it, just as Christ does the church, because we are members of his body. Therefore a man shall leave his father and mother and hold fast to his wife, and the two shall become one flesh. This mystery is profound, and I am saying that it refers to Christ and the church. However, let each one of you love his wife as himself, and let the wife see that she respects her husband."

The purpose of the husband and wife are different as in the beginning God assigned man and woman differing roles. Man was created to work and the woman was designed to help man in his tasks. Although their roles were different, they were both created in God's image and therefore, their roles were equal in value, neither role and responsibility was greater than the other.

In the New Testament, the roles of husband and wife are symbolic of Christ and His church. Christian men are to lovingly lay down their lives for their wives. They still maintain leadership as High Priest which is servant leadership, just as Christ serves the church. Husbands are not to demand obedience, but by their humility, guide. They are to honor their wives and not treat them any less than themselves but to lead and serve lovingly.

The Bible exalts womanhood in the home, and places great value on her. The wife's role from creation has not changed; although women have evolved in society and have become career-oriented and leaders in their own right, the Bible instructs women to love their husbands and children and to follow their husband's leadership with respect, choosing to submit to that leadership. Together with her husband, she is to provide the support needed with a positive attitude to maintain an environment of love and unity within the home. Men and women were created with distinct abilities to fulfill these biblical roles, and when husbands and wives follow the biblical pattern within the home and come together in unity they are considered *one* unit that will bring glory to God as a picture of Christ and His church.

Start seeing your marriage as a winning team; with continued practice, hard work, respect, and love, your team will overcome every challenge and obstacle that comes your way.

Start seeing your marriage as a winning team; with continued practice, hard work, respect, and love, your team will overcome every challenge and obstacle that comes your way. Do not allow temporary failures or lost battles to discourage you from pressing forward; you may have lost a battle or two, but together you will surely win the war! Teamwork in your marriage will bring you continuous victories. Learn to trust and depend on each other more. There's no "I" in team, but there is an "I" in win, and when each spouse makes a commitment to do their personal part to work together as a team, you will win.

Reflection Scriptures:

Ecclesiastes 4:9-12 (ESV):

"Two are better than one, because they have a good reward for their toil. For if they fall, one will lift up his fellow. But woe to him who is alone when he falls and has not another to lift him up! Again, if two lie together, they keep warm, but how can one keep warm alone? And though a man might prevail against one who is alone, two will withstand him—a threefold cord is not quickly broken."

Genesis 2:18 (ESV):

"Then the LORD God said, 'It is not good that the man should be alone; I will make him a helper fit for him.'"

Romans 15:5-6 (ESV):

"May the God of endurance and encouragement grant you to live in such harmony with one another, in accord with Christ Jesus, that together you may with one voice glorify the God and Father of our Lord Jesus Christ."

Reflection Questions:

1. List the strengths and weaknesses of each spouse.

_____

_____

_____

_____

_____

2. In what ways can you better work as a team?

_____

_____

_____

_____

_____

3. Identify any challenges your marriage is currently facing, and list ways of overcoming them together.

_____

_____

_____

_____

_____

_____

_____

Prayer: Father, thank you for the key of teamwork, and for joining us together to be teammates in marriage. Teach us how to contribute to our marriage in positive ways that will lead us to greater victories on our journey. In Jesus' name, Amen!

Key #4:

Intimacy and Sex (One Flesh)

Eros Love

n intimate relationship is an interpersonal relationship involving physical or emotional intimacy, and is characterized by romantic or passionate attachment or sexual activity.

Intimacy is probably one of the most misunderstood concepts in relationships. Somewhere down the line intimacy and sex became interchangeable words because many people believe they are one and the same; while intimacy may include sex, it involves so much more. Intimacy encompasses an entire way of being, acting, and thinking; it is a place of commitment, vulnerability, and trust. Everyone has a general desire to belong and to love, which is usually satisfied within an intimate relationship. Intimacy is when both spouses understand each other while simultaneously feeling understood. People can be married for years and never truly be intimate with each other because intimacy is more than an emotional, physical expression of love or passion; it is an internal connection between husband and wife that allows each other to speak without using words. In our relationship, we have learned how to communicate with each other regarding several matters without using words because of the quality time that we have spent together over the years. It's almost as if we have the same thinking pattern; and we can trust each other to make major decisions when either one of us are absent, knowing we will make a choice that is correct for our family when needed.

Intimacy is the art of deep connection, and it is best achieved through spending quality, dedicated time with the one you love. The Latin word for intimacy is *intimus* meaning "inmost". Regardless of how it is displayed, intimacy is two hearts speaking to each other through different modes of communication that uses all five senses. Through sight, hearing, touch, taste, and smell, a couple can enter into deeper times of passion and intimacy than they have ever experienced. Look into each other's eyes without talking and listen to hear each other's heart. Touch each other often and explore different ways while allowing your bodies to connect; get to know the shape of your spouse's body and even the unwanted marks that exist.

Just as a newborn baby knows the smell and taste of their mother because of the closeness and intimacy they share, husband and wife can create such a bond with each other from discovering more about their spouse through times of intimacy and connection using all of their senses.

Through taste and smell, you will also discover more about your spouse and a deeper awareness of each other will be heightened. Just as a newborn baby knows the smell and taste of their mother because of the closeness and intimacy they share, husband and wife can create such a bond with each other from discovering more about their spouse through times of intimacy and connection using all of their senses.

The activities that are done are not as important as the focused time spent appreciating your spouse for who he or she is, because time is the ultimate factor to intimacy. Many books have detailed other activities to strengthen intimacy within a marriage; looking into your spouse's eyes, times of hand holding, surprises, dating, talking, laughing, kissing, trying new things, verbally expressing your deep feelings and love for each other and connecting deeper about the things that matter most in the relationship.

Women often complain that they are lacking intimacy in their relationship. For some, it's feeling like not enough quality time is spent together, for others its feeling like the time spent with each other does not carry with it any deep meaning.

Most men categorize intimacy through their wife's appreciation of them and paying attention to their needs and wants like initiating of affection and sexual interactions. A husband's expression of deep emotion often comes through physical interaction or through the things they do or accomplish for their wives. Because men and women are wired differently when it comes to intimacy and sex, a lot of attention and compromise is needed in order to meet your spouse at a healthy middle ground. Martin Luther, German priest and scholar said, *"Let the wife make the husband glad to come home, and let him make her sorry to see him leave."* Many couples face difficulty in connecting because of acts of selfishness or division, which makes each person vulnerable to temptation. When either husband or wife can find himself or herself drawn into a deep sense of connection, understanding, desire, or satisfaction with someone who is not their spouse, it is a dangerous emergency that needs intervention and should not be taken lightly.

Intimacy is seldom an area individuals learn from their parents. Because deep intimacy is often a private interaction between husband and wife, couples approach this area based merely on their past experience with others or without any experience at all. The beautiful thing about intimacy is it has many levels. Just like the spiritual illustration of tabernacle worship in the Bible, intimacy with your spouse can be viewed from the "outer court", which is what everyone can see on the outside; to the "inner court", which is what your close friends or family may see, into the "holy of holies", which is reserved for just you, your spouse, and God. We often categorize intimacy only based on what everyone can see like the outer court, but deep intimacy is what takes place behind closed doors with you and your spouse—an opening of yourself so that your spouse can see deep within. Intimacy = "into-me-see".

When intimacy is genuine and consistent within the relationship, there is a natural flow and desire for sexual interaction. Sex is one of the most important keys within a marriage, as the sexual connection with your spouse is an integral factor in maintaining a happy and satisfying relationship. Couples often face challenges in this area because of time, frequency, health reasons, hidden expectations/desires, dissatisfaction, and the lack of communication, creativity or romance. In order to maintain a healthy sexual relationship, an investment in addressing the challenges should be of high priority. Sex was intended by God through marriage to be pleasurable and enjoyable; the scripture states: *"Let marriage be held in honor among all, and let the marriage bed be undefiled, for God will judge the sexually immoral and adulterous"* (Heb. 13:4, ESV).

Couples should feel free to embrace the gift of sex and embark on the journey of discovery and exploration with each other's bodies. Sex within the marriage brings a unity and bond with your spouse that is deeply spiritual as it joins you together as one, connecting physically, emotionally, and spiritually. *"Therefore a man shall leave his father and his mother and hold fast to his wife, and they shall become one flesh. And the man and his wife were both naked and were not ashamed" (Gen. 2:24-25 ESV).*

Shame should not exist within the sexual relationship between husband and wife. Couples can experience great liberation through maintaining open communication about their desires and expectations to avoid any shame, guilt, temptation, or any negative feelings that will push you further apart rather than bring you closer together. Be open and honest with each other about your feelings concerning the sexual relationship so that the comfort level will increase and your sexual experiences will become more pleasurable and satisfying.

The area of sexual dissatisfaction is one of the top five reasons for marital conflict and divorce. Past sexual experiences with other people, unexpressed desires or expectations, lustful tendencies, and negative habits are issues that create a void between husband and wife. Couples experiencing problems in these areas should tackle the issues as early as they are discovered to avoid the damaging effects they will have on the relationship.

Sex on its own is not enough to build a successful marriage. Many people use their sexual interactions to measure their relationship status, but a healthy marriage will exist beyond a physically or emotional exchange even though both components are needed for the marriage to have a healthy balance. Remember to have fun, enjoy each other, plan, communicate, be creative, and experiment. During sex, your goal is to make sure your wife/husband is satisfied and catered for to the best of your ability. Together you can begin a fresh new journey in your sexual relationship by taking the time to communicate about your sexual experiences and discuss each other's desires needs and ideas. Build a relationship with your spouse that makes stepping outside of the relationship for intimacy or sex impossible.

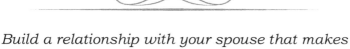

Build a relationship with your spouse that makes stepping outside of the relationship for intimacy or sex impossible.

Reflection Scriptures:

1 Corinthians 7:2-5 (ESV):

"But because of the temptation to sexual immorality, each man should have his own wife and each woman her own husband. The husband should give to his wife her conjugal rights, and likewise the wife to her husband. For the wife does not have authority over her own body, but the husband does. Likewise the husband does not have authority over his own body, but the wife does. Do not deprive one another, except perhaps by agreement for a limited time, that you may devote yourselves to prayer; but then come together again, so that Satan may not tempt you because of your lack of self-control."

Proverbs 5:19 (ESV):

"A lovely deer, a graceful doe. Let her breasts fill you at all times with delight; be intoxicated always in her love."

Reflection Questions:

1. List three ways you can improve your intimacy.

_____

_____

_____

_____

_____

_____

_____

_____

2. List your sexual expectations or desires (including ones you have not yet shared with your spouse). Discuss ways to explore them.

_____

_____

_____

_____

_____

3. Identify any intimacy or sexual challenges you are currently facing, and list ways of overcoming them together.

_____

_____

_____

_____

_____

_____

_____

Prayer: Dear Heavenly Father, thank you for the gift of intimacy and sex. Teach us how to appreciate each other through this marriage key, so that we grow in a deeper physical, spiritual, emotional connection with each other in Jesus' name, Amen!

Key #5:

Commitment (We're in This Together)

Pragma Love

9

"For better/for worse, for richer/for poorer, in sickness and in health, forsaking all others, till death do us part..." The vows that you made on your wedding day were a promise, a commitment.

Commitments are made by choice and are meant to be binding to the end of the agreed upon time; in the context of marriage, it's meant to last a lifetime. A friend of ours told us a story about a pastor who decided to officiate a wedding and remove these parts of the vow from the ceremony because they felt it produced "negative energy" and the ceremony should only include acknowledgement of positive things. While we understand the intention of the pastor, The truth is: life is filled with unforeseen circumstances; many of which we have no control over or can even see coming. The commitment made to your spouse through the vow is made with the understanding things will happen on this journey and no matter what comes your way, you are making a choice to stick with each other through the good, the bad, and the ugly. *Kemmy Nola of Amore Love for Life* quotes, *"We were designed to be caught by the covenant of marriage, when commitment wears thin. At such times, when we have trouble keeping our vows, our vows keep us."*

Commitment may not be viewed as an appealing word or concept, but it has a lot to do with the success of a marriage. It's not just about saying marriage vows or having a piece of paper that says "marriage license", but it's having the assurance you are in the ship together and your future is tied with the one you love. Relationships remain in limbo when there's a feeling the other person may not be around forever or when options or variables exist.

The commitment to your spouse is a choice to give up choices. While this might at first sound limiting, it actually brings great freedom and depth to your relationship—no longer does either person need to weigh options about other "potential" individuals, possibilities, or other ways of life that might bring "more happiness".

Once the vow is made, keep your eyes on your spouse and focus on making that commitment work. The two major stages of commitment are making the initial commitment, and ultimately keeping the commitment.

"Till death do us part" can sound so romantic, but it can also sound deadly. Regardless of the style of the marriage ceremony most couples still believe they are making a permanent commitment when they walk down the aisle and make their vow. Unfortunately, the divorce rate is between forty and fifty percent because most couples who marry don't think it will happen to them.

Clearly, the decision to divorce is not a "one size fits all" situation as various situations and reasons have brought many couples to this sad separation. Some couples made the decision to marry too young, too impulsively, too naively; while others were not psychologically mature enough to "forsake all others" or had other character flaws that were overlooked or not evident during courtship. Then there are others who just got bored or tired of trying to make it work; while others earnestly worked and gave their all to the marriage but their partner decided he or she wanted out – no marriage will be successful with an absent spouse. Still there are others who have no choice but to leave their marriage for their own safety.

In the book *The Case for Marriage* by Linda J. Waite and Maggie Gallagher, it is noted research has shown many marriages could be revived if the commitment is strong. Waite and Gallagher surveyed a large national sample of unhappily married couples and found after five years, three fifths of the formerly unhappy couples reported they were happy or quite happy. Sometimes it is simply the commitment to each other that carries a couple through the harder times, along with focused times of reconciliation, counseling, effort, and faith.

To love is a decision, and the "feeling" of love alone is not sufficient for a marriage. At some point (actually many points) husband and wife need to decide to love, even when they don't feel like it.

To love is a decision, and the "feeling" of love alone is not sufficient for a marriage. At some point (actually many points) husband and wife need to decide to love, even when they don't feel like it. Following up on your decision to love will be best supported by your actions of love toward your spouse: doing loving things for each other, speaking kindly and respectfully, and deciding over and over to pay attention to the relationship makes love rekindle. Too much energy is spent on falling in love, but we need to learn more how to stand in love. In the commitment to your marriage you stand in love, making an effort to give love rather than just receive it.

Couples who understand the essence of making a permanent commitment realize it's much more than just a decision not to divorce. It's a commitment to do the daily work of keeping the commitment alive within yourself and your marriage. It might even mean planning a lunch, dinner, or a short getaway in order to listen to each other's concerns. These simple actions and many more are practical ways to live out your commitment and keep your marriage vibrant, interesting, and exciting so temptations to make another choice don't even erupt.

Nowadays, some individuals struggle with commitment because they have seen or experienced many examples of broken promises within their homes or in their lifetime. It would almost appear as if commitments are invaluable and no longer carry the weight of integrity or trust. It is not enough to say you are committed to your marriage, and not behave in a manner that shows that commitment. Being committed to the marriage means you are committed to being an active part of the team; each spouse must realize commitment goes beyond just being faithful physically, but it also means being committed to the responsibilities that go along with the marriage relationship and the building and nurture of the household and family unit.

Some spouses have dealt with challenges of having the other spouse physically present in the home but disengaged, preoccupied, or uninterested in all that is happening within the home or with the children; while others have not committed to submitting to the needs and nurture of the other. Both require a deeper under-standing of how a commitment to the marriage goes deeper than the verbal vow made on the wedding day to being an active and contributing member of the team.

Commitment to each other becomes a shield of respect that penetrates the intrusion of any outside individuals or circumstances that would try to interfere with the bond between husband and wife. When both husband and wife keep a deep sense of honor and respect for the vow and devotion made to each other, it will be easier to overcome temptations. To devote yourself to your spouse "to the exclusion of all others" is a vow honorable not only to each other but onto God.

When a plane reaches a specific speed for takeoff and stopping for any reason is no longer possible, the pilot says, "I'm committed". The same should be true in a marriage--once you've gone down the aisle or runway and have made the vow, there should be a decision made within your heart that says stopping for any reason is no longer an option because "I am committed!"

When a plane reaches a specific speed for takeoff and stopping for any reason is no longer possible, the pilot says, "I'm committed". The same should be true in a marriage—once you've gone down the aisle or runway and have made the vow, there should be a decision made within your heart that says stopping for any reason is no longer an option because "I am committed!"

Marriages should not be entered into unadvisedly or without the proper counsel or consideration for the other person. If you are experiencing obstacles within your relationship that are jeopardizing your commitment to each other, seek the necessary help and assistance to try and work through the challenges. Invest the time and focus necessary to work on the areas of weakness in order to preserve the marriage and to experience the joy the marriage is intended to bring to both of you. While the key of commitment may sound like a lot of work and energy to be applied to your relationship, the fruit it produces will not only bless your marriage, but will be a precious gift for your family. A vow is made on the day of the wedding through passion and love, but the commitment is what will make your marriage stand the test of time.

Reflection Scriptures:

Numbers 30:2 (ESV):

"If a man vows a vow to the LORD, or swears an oath to bind himself by a pledge, he shall not break his word. He shall do according to all that proceeds out of his mouth."

Mark 10:8-10 (KJV):

"And they twain shall be one flesh: so then they are no more twain, but one flesh. What therefore God hath joined together, let not man put asunder."

Reflection Questions:

1. List three ways you have shown commitment to your marriage.

_____

_____

_____

_____

_____

_____

_____

2. In what ways have your vows been tested?

_____

_____

_____

_____

_____

_____

_____

3. Identify areas of improvement for your marriage.

_____

_____

_____

_____

_____

_____

_____

Prayer: Father, teach us how to honor our vows and commitment to each other in a manner that reflects your commitment to us. Deepen our love and respect for one another so that our bond will be unbreakable in Jesus' name. Amen

Key #6:

Forgiveness (Not For the Faint of Heart)

Agape Love

Forgiveness is the intentional and voluntary process by which a victim undergoes a change in feelings and attitude regarding an offense and lets go of negative emotions such as vengefulness, with an increased ability to wish the offender well.

The key of forgiveness is a special key within a marriage because while it is used for the benefit of the couple, it is a key used individually by each spouse. It has been said, "forgiveness is for you and not the other person". It is the true art of letting go. Being able to forgive and to let go of past hurts is a critical tool for your marriage. No relationship, especially a marriage, can be sustained over a long period of time without forgiveness. A person who holds onto old hurts, disappointments, betrayals, insensitivities, and anger risks wasting time and energy and will eventually lead into more hate and extreme bitterness. It is the lack of forgiveness or the feeling of not being forgiven that adds physical and mental strain within the relationship and a build up of distance between husband and wife.

Most people struggle with forgiveness. Let's face it: forgiveness can be painful. When a spouse faces betrayal or hurt of any form from the person they love, the challenge of overcoming resentment, bitterness, and anger is difficult to get over. Many people are living in a marriage for years and have not learned how to truly forgive or let go of the hurt and painful experiences of the past within their heart toward their spouse.

Quite truthfully, many spouses have not learned how to properly communicate about the pains of the experiences they have faced to bring the closure and healing needed in order to move past the mistakes or offenses that have affected the relationship. Regardless of where you are in the process of forgiveness, if it is not exercised within the marriage, it will create a void within the relationship that creates blockages emotionally, mentally, verbally, and physically. Author Robert Quillen said, *"A happy marriage is made up of two good forgivers."*

How do you forgive someone who was never supposed to hurt you in the first place? Why forgive them? What about all the damage to your marriage and family? The best answer is you must in order to bring the proper closure and move forward in the relationship. Jesus said in Matthew 6:14-15 (NIV): "If you forgive those who sin against you, your heavenly Father will forgive you. But if you refuse to forgive others, your Father will not forgive your sins."

In our own marriage we have battled with forgiveness and the task of learning how to move past hurtful situations and experiences. We realized through communicating and discussing the issues, along with making a commitment to working through the challenges, we were able to overcome the hurdles in our marriage we once faced. In the earlier stages of our marriage we focused so much on seeing our own way, trying to prove our own points to the extent we did not see where we personally were going wrong, and how we were allowing seeds of unforgiveness to take root in our relationship. As we witnessed the distance growing between us and the direction our lack of forgiveness was taking our relationship, we made a choice to work on the areas in our lives individually that hindered us from forgiving each other the way God truly forgives us of our sins and wrongdoings.

The lack of courage to forgive deepens the bondage of the heart, but a heart that forgives brakes through the strongest bars of imprisonment.

Many people struggle to forgive because we naturally go into defense-mode to justify our rights and our anger, but when we appropriately apply God's Word through scriptures such as, "Be ye angry and sin not: let not the sun go down upon your wrath" (Ephesians 4:26, KJV), we develop a more tender heart toward the one who needs to be forgiven. If we are honest, many of us are angry and sin for days, weeks, months, years, and many have lived and died without forgiving their spouse. The lack of courage to forgive deepens the bondage of the heart, but a heart that forgives brakes through the strongest bars of imprisonment.

Offenses, trials, betrayal, and calamity come along the journey to teach us the art of real forgiveness. Today, society's standards for marriage are a slap in the face to what God originally intended. When we decide not to forgive, we call it "irreconcilable differences", while God calls it unforgiveness. Forgiveness is a choice and each spouse has the power to choose whether or not to forgive. We make the decision to forgive, even if our emotions, feelings, and desires have not surrendered in obedience to God. As children of God, we are led by faith, not feelings. When we make decisions based upon feelings, we risk losing the true gift with which God has blessed us. Sometimes dusting off and cleaning up the gift truly allows us to see how valuable that gift is. The gift is your spouse!

Below are a few tips on how to exercise forgiveness within the relationship:

- Be open.

- Make a decision to forgive your spouse. Forgiveness will release you from many emotional, spiritual strongholds.

- Don't dwell on the images of the betrayal or hurt, rather think of a calming place or do something to distract you from those thoughts.

- Don't throw past errors or mistakes back in your spouse's face in future arguments or discussions.

- Don't seek revenge or retribution. It will only extend the pain.

- Accept you may never know the reason for the mistake.

- Remember forgiveness doesn't mean you condone the hurtful behavior.

- Be patient with yourself. Being able to forgive your spouse takes time. Don't try to hurry the process. Allow your heart to be free so you can learn to love and forgive again.

- If you continue to be unable to forgive or you find yourself dwelling on the betrayal or hurt, please seek professional counseling to help you let go and forgive.

Forgiveness is to be given and to be received, as everyone will need to forgive and be forgiven. Many times challenges arise because a spouse does not know how to ask for forgiveness. Below are a few tips on how to ask your spouse for forgiveness:

- Acknowledge the pain you've caused.
- Be willing to acknowledge your behavior and commitment to not hurting your spouse again by repeating the hurtful behavior.
- Accept the consequences of the action that created the hurt.
- Be patient with your spouse. Being able to forgive you often takes time. Don't dismiss your spouse's feelings of betrayal by telling your spouse to "get over it." Learn to be patient and know time heals some things, but not everything. The power of forgiveness not only frees you to love again, but also gives you back more than what was taken away.

Strengthen your marriage today by beginning to work on true forgiveness toward each other. Forgiveness is not easy, but it's right.

Reflection Scriptures:

Ephesians 4:32 (ESV):

"Be kind to one another, tender-hearted, forgiving one another, as God in Christ forgave you."

Luke 6:37 (ESV):

"Judge not, and you will not be judged; condemn not, and you will not be condemned; forgive, and you will be forgiven;"

Reflection Questions:

1. Have you been able to offer forgiveness to your spouse? List any outstanding issues that you have not forgiven them.

_____

_____

_____

_____

_____

_____

_____

2. In what ways have you hurt your spouse currently or in the past? Have you asked for forgiveness, and is this a reoccurring issue?

_____

_____

_____

_____

_____

_____

3. Write a plan together of how you will overcome challenges requiring forgiveness.

_____

_____

_____

_____

_____

Prayer: Dear Father, the key of forgiveness is an important key to our marriage, and we ask you to help us to forgive each other the way that you forgive us of our sins. Teach us how to work through challenges that require forgiveness in order to keep our marriage free from bitterness or resentment in Jesus' name. Amen.

Key #7:

Spiritual Unity/Prayer

(As For Me And My House, We Will Serve The Lord)

Agape Love

According to the Miriam Webster dictionary, "Spirituality is defined as the sensitivity or attachment to religious values." The key of spiritual unity within a marriage is mainly described as the religious and moral values the couple shares.

Religious beliefs play an important role within a marriage because it incorporates the moral compass and approach to decision-making and lifestyle choices each individual makes. For a couple to face life and the many challenges together, they must be on the same page spiritually. Now being on the same page spiritually does not necessarily mean both of you express yourselves the exact same way; nor does it suggest that you copy how the other spouse practices their religious disciplines. Being on the same page means husband and wife are traveling together in the same direction concerning their faith and religious beliefs/values.

At the beginning of this book we spoke about having a "captain" on this ship called marriage and the navigator for life we are referring to is our Heavenly Father through the Holy Spirit. For your marriage to remain strong, you must begin to see yourself and each other the way God sees you, and depend on His guidance and direction to lead you along the journey. We believe the declaration, "Whom God has joined together, let no man put asunder." In that, we agree God ultimately joins two people together for love and to fulfill His ultimate purpose in their lives.

It is not by coincidence that you and your spouse have met. The children you have birthed, the relationship that you have built, and the example of love and unity that has been expressed through your marriage is indeed part of a greater purpose being fulfilled. Spiritual unity within your marriage means worshipping together and praying together.

Humans were created by God to worship, therefore it becomes a natural part of our design. Each spouse individually has a "worship gene", whether they were raised by their parents to observe specific religious values, or whether they don't apply a specific religion to their lifestyle, the fact remains: each person will worship someone or something. The goal is to have a clear understanding of where each person is in their spirituality and join together to travel the journey of faith. When husband and wife are joined as one flesh, they are not only joined physically but spiritually as well, hence maintaining the spiritual lifestyle together for the household now becomes an important part of the relationship.

Christian worship is a lifestyle lived in honor to God. The lifestyle of a worshipper includes reading the Bible, praying, fasting, serving others, fellowship with other believers (through local church and/or community involvement), and obedience to the commandments and teachings of God regarding lifestyle choices. Spiritual unity with your spouse begins when both of you agree to incorporate worship lifestyle choices within your marriage. Some couples are challenged by different views about denominational issues, where they attend church, ministry involvement, and devotional practices. To overcome these challenges, the couple should commit to begin reading scriptures and praying together so the unity can begin first within the relationship and then be extended to external involvement. Being on the same page in this area will create the unity and example needed to raise children and guide them in a Christian household.

Prayer is the most unused arsenal in a married couple's artillery, yet so much of what couples face in their relationship requires the wisdom and guidance of the Holy Spirit.

Prayer is the most unused arsenal in a married couple's artillery, yet so much of what couples face in their relationship requires the wisdom and guidance of the Holy Spirit. Because marriage is truly a spiritual experience of two people becoming one, the key of spiritual unity and prayer should never be overlooked. The power of agreement through prayer unites two people in a way that changes their respect for the other, and creates a bond that becomes unbreakable. For a couple to walk the journey of marriage, there must be an agreement, "Can two walk together, except they be agreed?" (Amos 3:3, KJV) An agreement means setting aside differences, compromising in areas to bring peace to a situation, and resolving together we are going to move forward despite the challenges we may face.

Society is populated because of man and women procreating, but communities strive because of the types of families that exist within it.

Christian couples are often faced with the challenge of maintaining unity within the home. We firmly believe while personality clashes and emotional or communication challenges may exist, marriages are under spiritual attack. The breakdown of family values has impacted our communities and our world in the most catastrophic of ways; and in order to build back the respect and strength of the family unit, it begins with husband and wife. Society is populated because of man and women procreating, but communities strive because of the types of families that exist within it. Families that apply love and moral respect within and outside of the home for their neighbors will begin a chain of love and respect within the community.

Together you can start the rebuilding process through prayer. Studies have shown the old adage, "A family/ couple who prays together stays together," actually has a lot of truth to it. This is especially true if couples have a shared faith and invest in the spiritual aspect of their lives regularly.

Why is prayer so important within a marriage?

- Prayer helps to build the faith to believe things will be better during difficult times.
- Prayer opens the door for forgiveness when a partner does something wrong.

- Prayer helps a couple stay strong and act in love toward one another when they are not feeling particularly loving toward one another.

- Prayer helps a couple to realign themselves with the will of God for their relationship.

- Prayer helps a couple feel vulnerable to one another.

- Prayer is another way for a couple to spend quality, intimate time together.

- Together a couple can go to God with requests. Praying for the requests of each other and requests for the family.

"You may ask me for anything in my name, and I will do it" (John 14:14).

Not only do we submit to the guidance of the Holy Spirit over our marriage and our children daily, but also we invite God into our relationship. We ask Him to help us be the husband/wife He designed us to be. In addition, we bring before Him struggles, decisions, and situations that exist between us asking for His help and healing. Praying for your marriage and your role as a spouse is the best possible thing you can do. In her book, *The Power of a Praying Wife,* Stormie Omartian says, "Talking to God about your husband is an act of love. Prayer gives rise to love, love begets more prayers, which in turn gives rise to more love."

Not only can prayer protect, heal, and help your marriage, but it's also an incredible way to connect on an intimately spiritual level through incorporated times of prayer. Through this special time together, you will begin to see the deep intimacy, love, and respect you share. Prayer with your spouse will lead to prayer with your children, and God will continue to bind your marriage and your family in a way that His presence will continue to fill your house.

Prayer with your spouse will lead to prayer with your children, and God will continue to bind your marriage and your family in a way that His presence will continue to fill your house.

The journey of marriage comes with a mirage of emotions and challenges; but traveling with your spouse through spiritual unity will help you to overcome every season and stage of life your marriage faces. Using the key of spiritual unity simply reinforces the saying, "United we stand; divided we fall." With God as your "Captain" and your spouse as your spiritual partner for the journey, your marriage and your family will last leaving a legacy for generations to come.

Reflection Scriptures:

James 5:16 (ESV):

"Therefore, confess your sins to one another and pray for one another, that you may be healed. The prayer of a righteous person has great power as it is working."

Philippians 4:6–7 (NIV):

"Do not be anxious about anything, but in every situation, by prayer and petition, with thanksgiving, present your requests to God. And the peace of god, which transcends

all understanding, will guard your heart and your mind in Christ Jesus."

Reflection Questions:

1. Do you and your spouse walk in spiritual unity? If yes, list how; if no, list the reasons why.

    _____

    _____

    _____

    _____

    _____

    _____

2. List ways to strengthen the spiritual unity together with your spouse.

    _____

    _____

    _____

    _____

_____

_____

_____

3. Create a marriage prayer list and devotional
   plan together.

_____

_____

_____

_____

_____

_____

Prayer: Dear Father, thank you for the key of prayer. We identify that you are the captain of our ship and we need you to guide us along the journey of our marriage. We submit our relationship and our family into your hands; teach us how to be Godly spouses to each other and to commit to praying for each other and our relationship. We recognize we need you on our journey and our ultimate success is in you. Amen.

Conclusion

*N*othing great is built without a vision, plan, and hard work; such is the same with your marriage. What is the vision for your marriage? What is the plan you are using to see the vision become a reality? Are you making the necessary investments in order to make your marriage work?

The weather and seasons will change as you both travel along this ship of marriage, but if you apply and maintain the necessary love keys to your marriage, you will learn how to weather every storm that comes your way and enjoy the times of sunshine and warmth your journey will bring.

The love keys we have shared with you in this book are keys that will not only strengthen your relationship, but will bring you closer together as a couple. The responsibility is now yours to use the keys to unlock any closed doors in your marriage you have either not opened or you have closed in your relationship.

Friendship Key – Build the friendship with your spouse.

Communication Key – Speak, listen, and learn.

Teamwork Key – Your spouse is your teammate/life's partner; begin to work together as a team.

Intimacy & Sex Key – Connect deeply and explore each other unashamedly.

Commitment Key – Make a choice to honor your vow.

Forgiveness Key – Offload the baggage that might be weighing down your ship and forgive the past and move forward together.

Spiritual Unity & Prayer – A couple/family that prays together stays together. Join together spiritually and experience a deeper level of intimacy and faith not only for your marriage, but for your family.

Marriage is such a beautiful gift to mankind and without the proper support, influences, and perspective we fail to see how our spouse has been a blessing given to us by God. While every couple has their own DNA, our prayer is that these foundational love keys will inspire you to invest in your relationship and ultimately be a source of strength to your marriage. Our prayer is your marriage will be a testimony of love, commitment, and applied principles that will be an example to your family, friends, and neighbors so the beauty of marriage can be restored in our society to the way God intended it to be: a lifelong legacy of respect, honor, and love.

"A successful marriage requires falling in love many times, always with the same person."

– Mignon McLoughlin

Notes

Introduction/Preface

C.S. Lewis, *"The Four Loves"*, (Geoffrey Bles, 1960)

Chapter - Communication

Dr. Adrian Rogers, *"Communication in Marriage"*, (Crosswalk.com, August 27, 2003)

Dr. Gary Chapman, *"The Five Love Languages"*, (Northfield Publishing, 1995)

Chapter - Teamwork

Dr. Phil McGraw, *"Financial and Marital Harmony"*, (Money Article)

Fawn Weaver, *"The Happy Wives Club"*, (Thomas Nelson Publishers, December 9, 2013)

Chapter - Commitment

Linda J. Waite and Maggie Gallagher, *"The Case for Marriage"*, (First Broadway Books, November 2001)

Chapter - Spiritual Unity/Prayer

Stormie Omartian, *"The Power of a Praying Wife"*, (Harvest House Publishers, 2014)

CPSIA information can be obtained
at www.ICGtesting.com
Printed in the USA
LVHW041937080219
606967LV00012B/113

7 LOVE KEYS
TO A SUCCESSFUL
MARRIAGE

Marriage is a wonderful experience and is best appreciated when husband and wife are enjoying the journey together. In *7 Love Keys to a Successful Marriage*, Shawn & Caleen Howard share principals based on the Greek expressions of love for building intimacy to help today's couple tap into solid truths for a lasting marriage. With over 16 years of personal and professional experience helping couples, they have combined foundational components in this book to further their mission in motivating and inspiring couples to stay together and embrace God's gift of marriage to mankind.

Embark on an exciting new journey today with your spouse and discover *7 Love Keys to a Successful Marriage* that will motivate, inspire, and unlock the hidden treasures that exist in your relationship. "Till death do us part" is not a life sentence but a beautiful love story. It's time to start loving!

About the Authors
Bishop Shawn & Pastor Caleen Howard are the Lead and Executive Pastor's of Life Changers Church in the City of Toronto. Together they serve as community leaders through Life Coaching, Motivational Speaking, Consulting, and Outreach Services to assist individuals and families live in the abundance of their God-given purpose. While Shawn & Caleen work diligently in ministering to others bringing hope, transformation, and inspiration, they recognize that their family is top priority, and ministry begins first at home. They are the proud parents of three beautiful children - Malachi, Caleb, and Jordynn-Renée.

For bookings visit: www.The-Howards.com

ISBN 978-1-4984-3856-8
90000

9 781498 438568

xulon
PRESS